Courage, Tears & Butterflies

A Woman's Journey to Self

NAOMI GEORGE

BookLeaf Publishing

India | USA | UK

Made with ❤ on the BookLeaf Publishing Platform
www.bookleafpub.in
www.bookleafpub.com

Dedication

For my children, Tamara and Zane,
you are my gifts from the Universe.
My forever-babies,
I love you then, now and forever.

Preface

This collection of poems is inspired by **"Mother Goddess —Birthed by Covid-19,"** which I wrote in 2020 during the pandemic. I was alone in Pune with my two children, then ten and seven years old. Their father was in Hong Kong and could not return as countries had sealed their borders. At forty, I found myself railing against a world I no longer understood. The weight of being both guardian and mother, protector and angel to my children pressed heavily upon me. Those two months confined with my exuberant, bewildered children in an apartment we couldn't leave, were profoundly difficult.

Yet, paradoxically, this period birthed the woman I would become. I had to dig deep for strength and, above all, hope. One night, after putting the children to bed, I sat at the dining table and wrote "Mother Goddess: Birthed by Covid-19" in a single sitting. It emerged from my gut and the sinews of my heart. Raw, it captured everything I was feeling then and honors that pivotal part of my journey.

Since 2020, my life has changed irrevocably, and I've evolved into the woman I was always meant to become. That journey began in Pune with the writing of this poem. I didn't know then that it would be like a butterfly's wings, causing ripples that would forever transform my life and identity.

I always wanted a home for my "Mother Goddess," and when I saw the 21-day poetry challenge by Bookleaf Publishing, I leapt at the opportunity. These poems reflect my transition from caterpillar to butterfly—my self-actualization—hence "butterflies" in the title. "Courage and tears" because no journey, especially one of transformation, is possible without both.

Gender and womanhood are strong themes throughout. I explore what it means to be a woman, as well as the social definitions of "man" and "woman." A current of spirituality runs through the collection as well—I am spiritual, deriving my strength from this place, and this essence permeates the work.

In the end, this collection represents my transformation over the past five years. I am deeply grateful for the journey: family, my children, friends, my co-parenting partner, and all who have walked alongside me.

Acknowledgements

This section can only begin with my mother, Sharon George. Mummy, I am because you are. You have stood beside me like a fierce lioness, wise-woman, and loving mother, while also being my friend. Ahead of your times, brave with formidable strength, it is your shoulders I stand on. "In Darkness With My Mother" was written for you. Thank you for standing by me through it all, and for allowing me freedom to find my own way. For me there can never be any other mother figure. It is you entirely. I am forever grateful that I picked you to be my mother. I love you with all my heart.

My father, Mathew George - thank you, Daddy, for unconditional love. Gentle and caring, you loved me every day, steadfast in your presence - no matter my escapades, my choices that you did not necessarily understand - you have always loved me. I have felt cherished by you and, always, like I was enough for you. Thank you, Daddy, for everything. I love you with all my heart.

Itisha Peerbhoy, my blue turquoise. I have always felt that if my life were a tapestry, you would be the brightest blue thread woven throughout. Friends since college, I cannot imagine my life without you. You are one of my life's greatest treasures. Thank you, Izzy, for the laughter, the love, the tears, and the conversation! For standing by me and with me through the gates of hell, in sunshine and rain, tipsy and sober. The poem "Sisterhood" is inspired by you, my beautiful friend. Love you always and forever.

Nihal George, my brother, my joy. You have always celebrated me, Nihal. You have made me feel seen and have shown up for me, bringing your large heart and generosity of spirit to every one of my key milestones. My first book, to when I hosted TEDxWoman, waiting patiently for three hours for the show to start, the only one who came, even though I was not speaking, only hosting - you came for me. For the love, the celebration, the joy you bring me, thank you. I love you with all my heart, and I am so tremendously grateful that I journey with you as sister in this life.

Gudrun Seth, my forever friend. For holding up the mirror to me and loving me no matter what the mirror showed, with your fierce love and counsel, I thank you. From college till now, I am so grateful we get to be wrinkly and fabulous together. Thank you also for being so gentle with your comments when you read this collection and for your thoughtful edits. Love you, G!

Masume Ali Khan, my intrepid friend, wise and sexy, strong and brave, for all the wisdom, the delight, the heart and support, thank you. When I have faltered, I have looked ahead and seen you - bravely and whole-heartedly living your life as single-parent and woman - with appetite, ambition, and zest - never giving in, staying vibrationally high. You have been the woman I have channeled on dark days. Gratitude for you, 'mutton biriyani' to my 'rasam' :).

For the gift of Sisterhood I have received from my girlfriends. I am forever grateful to all these women for being in my life. For bringing me joy, love, support, and meaning. You make my life rich - Kavita Pai, Tanya Alexander, Mandira Kumar, Shalini Makar, Kakoli Das, Sneha Parihar, Sandeep Johal, Salina Gilhotra, Pooja Shankar, Nausheen Jacob, Divya Chakola. The poem Sisterhood is for you.

Finally women I consider 'light-bearers' of the Earth, from whom I have learnt so much, received knowledge and wisdom. Thank you for the illumination: Oprah Winfrey, Esther Perel, Brene Brown!

Mother Goddess Birthed by Covid-19

I am the Mother Goddess, the one who Cares,
Terrible in her ferociousness,
Wrathful in her rage.

I am the Mother Goddess,
the one who Protects,
the one who must be Hunter & Gatherer,
the one who must be cook, cleaner and minder,
I am the Mother Goddess, Savage in her Care.

I am the Mother Goddess
who grew up a Princess and inherited a Kingdom,
I am the Mother Goddess who must Rule without her
consort.
The Mother Goddess who will raise her Children,
around the sound of her Command
the energy of her Action, the Doing of her deeds.

I am the Mighty.
The onion slicing, chocolate-cake baking,
N-95 mask wearing,
dal making, pot scouring, kitchen scrubbing, dispenser of
hugs.

The sop to tears, the arms to her children.

A whisky swilling, cigarette smoking, Mother Goddess
am I,
one who leads her Charge
through deadly infectious Battle,
One the World was not prepared for, least of all She.

I am the Mother Goddess who Rages,
who wins each day and must rise to do it again, day after
day,
whose tears stain her pillow,
whose smile must kindle her children, whose love must
uphold them.

I am the Mother Goddess with clay feet,
the one who gets it Wrong. The one who gets it Right.
I am She who is formidable. I am She who will endure. I
am She who weeps,
whose Spirit will triumph,
I am the Mother to my children,
who may choose to love me or revile me.

I am the Mother Goddess who will lead her Charge,
raise them Free to be Beings of their Own,
who if they choose to never look back will accept,
because she Reigned as she knew how.

I am Shakti, I am Kali, I am Mother Mary
I am my children's Mother.

Diamonds in the Water

I choose
diamonds in the water,
Bianco on ice,
raspberry smoke, crushed petals, sea salt, and honey.

I choose,
bare feet on grass,
sunsets of orange, pink, and gold,
velvet night, stars burning,
orb of moon.

I choose,
magic and potions,
mystery of ancient temples, fragrant agarbati,
frankincense.

I choose the wild ride of a wild heart,
the journey,
I choose.

When a Woman Leaves

When a woman leaves,
she leaves ruptured,
weighted and freed by her choice.
She's paid the price for freedom,
the price in Guilt.
How Dare she choose Herself?

Guilt lays with her at night
and shadows her mornings.
In the tears of her children,
she feels the terrible lancing,
Guilt's relentless gnawing.

Her children cry and she weeps,
she Chose Herself.
This is the price: Crushing,
one-of-a-kind,
that only women pay.

Yet,
Through fog of Doubt and Fear,
as she builds Life anew,
she stays True to Herself.
In time,

Guilt eases its stranglehold demand;
in its place Peace,
and as the children learn to smile again,
she can Breathe again.

Her children's hands clasped in hers, she walks Tall.
Yes, she dared to choose Herself,
knowing the all-consuming Price down to her bones.
She shattered the ancient narrative,
the perpetual litany of two-thousand years:
'a mother's selflessness, her eternal sacrifice';
she Smashed that story into smithereens,
she Chose Herself.

This is the Cross, this is the Legacy
of a woman who leaves.
A new birthright for her children,
one where they are True to themselves.
A talisman for soaring,
Freedom to be Selfish, because their Mother dared.

This is my Cross, this is my Legacy, this is my Gift.

Butterflies Divine

Butterfly Divine, reminder of good spirits,
when footsteps falter and doubt looms large,
when my spirit is tired, and hope is far,
then Butterfly Divines flit across my path.

Unexpected,
they lift my heart, dancing delight,
crimson rose, bluebottle blue, sulphur and yellow,
bigger than big, smaller than small, they dance ahead,
ephemeral grace and glimmer.

Enraptured, uplifted, they dance for me, I'm sure.
A reminder,
good Spirits are with me,
divinity close.

Renewal flows into my being,
joy stirs in my veins,
my spirit grows light, feet lift in hope,
faith once more.

Growth and transformation is the Journey,
but all along,
Butterfly Divines to light the way.

Holding On Letting Go

Holding on to what once was,
grieving what could have been,
holding on to what once was
the novel Whole.

Paradoxical grief as new chapters emerge,
holding on tight to what was,
afraid to allow a new story,
grieving what could have been,
even as new pages form,
the writing pointing,
to what could be for me.

Holding onto memory,
of what was once so dear,
once the whole world, maybe even the universe,
now, inexplicably, stardust -
the novel whole becoming,
a chapter, perhaps a footnote.

Am I allowed,
permission to open clutching fingers?
Unfurl hands marked with grief, stigmata,
open them to a new galaxy,

a different ending, a novel new,
one that could come fairytale true.

Holding on Letting Go, so I may smile once more.

Sunbeam

Kakoli calls me sunbeam,
sometimes she calls me peacock,
because I wear indigo-blue eyeliner
and shimmer eyeshadow.

It is true, I am peacock.
I spread my tail feathers, frequently dance
in iridescent blue green,
drenched in Life or the Moment,
high on conversation with the Universe.

Dopamine dressing,
I dress the way I want to feel,
and tell the Universe,
'now deliver Rain'!

The Universe colludes
with shimmery vibrations of blue-green hue,
it loves this dancing vibe.
Together we tango, salsa and cha-cha,
the Universe and I.

Courage is a Heart Word

A heart willing to be laid bare,
pierced and shredded,
not once but one thousand times,
maybe more, is courage.

Bathed in tears of trying,
lacerated with loving,
bruised from dreaming,
courage braves the booing of the crowd,
the weight of other's opinions,
 to stay true to the quiet call within.

Courage stands alone at crossroads,
vulnerable and unknowing,
yet strides forward anyway.
Stays on the path,
thorny,
unmapped,
led by quiet whispers of a steadfast heart.

Courage is life moving from fear to living;
though one thousand tears are shed,
agony and fear,
courage burns, a stubborn flame

that honors inner knowing;
is a life aligned to inner truth— courage is heart!

12

Dark Night of the Soul

What shall I do
what shall I be?
Frenetic scrambling. Purpose, where are you?
What shall I do, what shall I be,
this desperate search for Meaning.

Raging with questions, silent with despair
heavy numbness,
burning with hunger,
restless, seeking,
starvation of the soul.

What shall I do
what shall I be?
Don a uniform
be a traffic cop, eclairs in my pocket
sticky in the sun.
Wear an avatar,
seduce; be an adulteress.

Create,
honeycomb and raspberry, dark chocolate cake,
baker divine?
Make jewelry! Red brick and yellow bumble beads,

paper mache and silver.
Dance! Play the piano, garden, write a song
What shall I do, what shall I be?!

Tears fall, the way is long
misty, foggy grey,
there is no light in the dark night of the soul.
Alone, silent
belly crawling towards the light,
must all be lost before it is won?

Oh, endless night of endless time,
blinded, heeding only whispers of the soul,
step by uncertain step,
till at last through twilight haze,
glimmers of light.

This is no crisis, this endless night,
the dark night of the soul.
Layers are shed in this place
snake like,
past selves discarded,
in pain and anguish, blood and tears,
in wild howls under silvery ancient moons.

Salvation's path, the search for meaning,
is the Awakening that can never begin,

without the cries, the aching hunger,
the seeking of the soul.

So, journey into the night Valiant heart,
Your dark night is the other side of light.

Joy

Joy is yellow sunshine, a fat sunflower,
a note of love from my brother.
Joy is petal yellow,
golden rose from a street vendor.

Joy is sitting on my table,
it feels like love,
smells like happy.
sounds like laughter
joy is yellow.

For my girl, my forever wish, for daughters of the Earth

Cusp of sixteen, my beautiful girl,
long legs and hope,
soft brown eyes,
tender like a shoot, a rose just blooming,
soft with dew, bright with possibility,
my beautiful girl.

What can I give her
my bramble rose,
so she may always bloom,
be happy,
smile in the sun.

Freedom—
to reach for stars, spread her wings,
to get it wrong, to get it right.
Freedom from fear,
to live boldly, curiously,
to dance, to sing, uncaring of voices

that clip her wings.

Freedom to delight in being a woman,
to embrace beauty and pleasure,
free from shame,
knowing: *You are enough, my Tamara.*

This is my prayer, my hope
for my daughter and all daughters of the earth.
You are enough,
more, much more than you know.

May our girls run free,
swoop, glide,
sit at boardrooms, crunch numbers,
climb mountains, nest at home,
walk barefoot in the grass, win awards or not.
May they be happy,
being whom they choose to be.

What shall I give my girl, my bramble rose,
freedom, my darling,
freedom to be You.

For my son, my forever wish, for sons of the earth

My second born, my son,
the one I baby,
the one who needs me so.
The one who come to nestle,
who loves to cuddle still.

I see you,
twelve, still a boy.
Even as you stand on cusp
of breaking voice,
first facial down,
in you, I see
softness, care.

Blessed with talent—
Football star,
track and field athlete born.
Medals galore,
sweat and glory,
Zane Mathews, superstar.

Yet I wish,
amid this testosterone rush

of competition and prize,
you stay kind.
Hero on the field,
yet gentle at the core.

May you never fall prey
to the lie that claims
men cannot cry, show tenderness, or weep.
May you embrace the hug,
claim your compassion,
stand unafraid in vulnerability.

May you know
it's ok to be weak;
on days you cannot be strong,
you're still a man.

May you respect all kind,
see beyond binary.
Play,
wear purple, yellow, orange, and pink.
Sing ballads,
write poems, play the ukulele,
sketch;
beyond electric guitar, spikes, football, and drums,
dare to venture.

Unbox,
dance like a butterfly, sting like a bee,
wash dishes.
Kick like Ronaldo, run like Bolt,
wield a broom, make lunch-box sandwiches.

May you, my son, and all sons of the earth,
in pursuit of Alpha,
never lose the knowing:
that boys thrive on tenderness,
and men are born to feel.

Content

My children are home,
cricket is on,
Sunday afternoon.

Time is slow, drowsy, replete,
sighs,
a dog warm, splayed in the sun,
purrs,
a cat on a purple silk cushion.
Marmalade on toast,
a fat teapot,
afternoon quiet, time feels content.

My son on his ukulele
strumming,
my daughter in her room
buried in physics, distracted by Pinterest.

My heart feels a gurgle, my children are home.
Sunday afternoon,
time is slow,
feels full, nourished, fed,
time is not empty.

Sisterhood

If life were a Turkish kilim,
an Afghan rug,
a Persian carpet or Indian dhurrie,
brightly patterned,
hand knotted,
warp and weft intertwined,
threads of silk and wool,
colour rich, vibrant,
woven into stages of a woman's life,
what might they tell?

Threads of scented jasmine,
sweet and pure for girlhood,
parrot green for vitality, growth, fertility.
Marigold orange, yellow for motherhood,
hibiscus red for womanliness,
Kali black for Shakthi, female power.

The brightest thread though,
woven through,
shimmering, laughing,
naughty with secrets,
deep with care,
wet with tears, tender with compassion,

the thread of sisterhood,
turquoise blue.

Pigtailed girl to silver-haired wise woman,
through all woman's seasons,
runs the turquoise thread,
upholding, uplifting,
eternally weaving,
gift of sisterhood.

Woman within my Mother

I fought for Her,
Woman within my Mother.
I sensed her disquiet,
knew her dissatisfaction
at being flattened into only role of Mother.

What of appetite for life,
one beyond caregiving and love?
What of dance, song and play,
French perfume and lace,
must they be forgotten?

What of Purpose, entirely her own?
Ambition, dreams,
the human need
to fully bloom, know her all,
be the highest vision
of her highest Self?

Woman within my Mother,
I made space for you.
Gave you time, so you may never fade,
and I forget, who I am,
without role of Mother.

Lavender Eyeshadow for Breakfast

Up at six, crack of dawn,
lunch boxes,
vitamins, water bottles, instructions,
dash to the bus,
kisses at the door for my children.

Bleary-eyed,
rested - perhaps un-rested,
it doesn't matter. The day has begun,
the hamster's wheel is spinning.
To the gym, Surya namaskar, breathwork,
intentional start, wellness over bed.

Dicing, slicing, menu-planning,
the rice is over, bread must be bought,
again!
Clocking in at work, presentations, meetings,
wait a minute,
tea-time snacks?!

Corn on the cob at 4pm,
a broken toe!
Pediatric visit after-school,

work meeting from the doctor's clinic,
thank God for Zoom, Microsoft, Google meet.

And so, before the mad dash of day
between breakfast and ten AM,
lavender eyeshadow, mascara,
make-up ritual,
for my inner woman.

After-bath oil, Indian rose, lime and oudh,
sweep of blush, raspberry lips
perfume,
so, I may feel like woman
even if she's on a hamster's wheel.

In Darkness with my Mother

I remember,
a time dark.
Lost,
unable to see,
unable to feel,
broken-hearted, spirit crushed,
devoid of energy.

Wounded
it felt then, beyond repair.
Lost,
felled to the ground,
I came home to you, mother.

You saw my darkness,
saw it in my vacant eyes,
my spirit dead.
You knew, I was not I.

You let me be.
Lioness to her cub, you watched over me.
Mother-like, you stayed,
Never once accusing,

"Will the children be OK?"
Never once admonishing,
"Become OK, your children need you!"

You stayed with me in the Dark,
 you knew,
the Light was mine to find,
you allowed me my dark,
you loved me in the dark.

A Woman Who Loves

When a woman loves
she gives her heart.
Joyfully given,
not in pieces or quarters,
not one ventricle,
transactional,
but all four,
spirit, center and emotion
her heart is given.

Not for safe keeping,
nor for completeness
or belonging.
An offering, a gift, her heart given,
Radha to Krishna,
Mother Mary to Son of God,
Parvathi and Shiva.

Divine love, loves forever,
no matter presence of the other,
alone or together,
it does not matter,
her heart will always love
the ones she has loved.

She is no silly girl
or lost woman.
She is one who loves,
Anahata,
she knows,
capacity of the heart.
Deep ocean wide, sweeping blue skies
expansive, massive, Universal-
capacity of the heart.

What could have been
a love story and was not,
will always be a love story;
all she once loved,
all whom she loves today,
live in her heart,
such is the love
of a woman who loves.

Alpha Male

Lean,
mean killer machine,
authoritative,
the voice in the room.
Presence.

Decisive, incisive, made of steel,
unbreakable.

Charming,
articulate: news, history, sport—
subject matter expert,
musician and poet.
Desirable to men, desirable to women.
Leader of the pack—
available to few, known to all,
alpha male.

Strong,
armored,
no weakness permitted—
bulletproofed against emotion.
In place by six years old,
impenetrable shield,

defense against tears or need.

Trained by fathers strong in Blue,
maybe beaten, left alone,
uncelebrated,
to learn, to earn
those worthy stripes—
affection and validation.

Deals to close,
the world to save—
switched on, in pursuit
of glory, respect, power.
Money, success, wife, family.
Perfection, status,
respect for the alpha male.

Leader of the pack—
they never told you
you will walk alone,
and when you need tenderness most,
you will instead choose
nights with Black Label, cigarette ashes,
weights in the gym, triathlon, golf, and protein.

Not knowing what is wrong,

why you weep,
when you have it all.

34

An Alpha Female's Choice

Yes, alpha male, you are hero—
but what of females
in your story?

Are you
the sole plot and narrative?

Is your female co-star
a line below your headline,
getting you coffee,
one step behind
your ambition, dash, and swagger?

Will you pause to listen,
ask, "What can I do for you today?"
Will you, alpha male,
see her weariness, show tenderness?

Hold her tired self—
want to be her joy,
place her center,
not as trophy or goddess,
but as friend and equal partner.

Oh, alpha male—
I am not sure
an alpha female would choose
inequity,
brawn over heart,
division of labor,
your persona,
your reflected glory.

For her,
a different man—
one unafraid to cry,
without armor,
with courage in vulnerability.
One who celebrates her, as she celebrates him.
One who takes her hand,
to walk together, not ahead.

When a woman is alpha,
grounded on her feet,
she chooses not alpha,
but man as equal partner.

She co-writes the story,
weaving a narrative
where she and he create
together.

Healing

I walked thirteen thousand steps in evening dusk,
twilight, and break of day—every day.

Under trees, on grass, by the lake,
with friendly bougainvillea, Bird of Paradise,
bottlebrush, bamboo, gulmohar, and jacaranda.

Flowers nodded to me, smiling as I walked.
They knew
I was on step one thousand
of thirteen thousand.

I saw kindness in leaves, understanding in barks of trees.
My aching heart, heavy spirit—they held for me.

When I rested my palm on the Egyptian Cottonwood
Tree,
it knew my silent cry.

The birds, the trees, the flowers,
butterflies who came to see me—
all knew my steps, my repeated path,
and held space for me.

They watched over me, never asking why,
as I questioned, wept, railed, and ranted,
wondered
what was wrong with me,
tormented
by my chosen path.

I poured my all to the trees,
wept with bamboo,
was miserable under jacaranda,
scared, lonely, anxious—
I fled to the trees.

They held me up, loved me through it all.
Thirteen thousand steps,
three hundred and sixty-five days,
and three years—
they walked with me,
tending wounds,
until I bled no more,
and my steps were light once more.

Mighty Rain Wood Tree,
you, whom I love so,
my sanctuary when weary.
You who stood resolute
when my strength faltered—

beneath your sweeping branches
of silent understanding, unspoken counsel, and ancient
wisdom—
I am healed.

Gratitude

If I had lived,
and never been alive,
sleep-walked through my days,
afraid to risk,
dare to dream,
step into the ring,
fail or feel,
empty would my life have been.

For the one hundred dreams I have dreamed,
will dream again;
the agony and ecstasy,
heart split wide open,
years of self-doubt,
the questions within,
I thank you, Universe.

For the roles bestowed as gift of life,
the gamut of feeling in woman, mother, daughter, friend,
lover, sister -
I thank you.

For my seeking soul, egotistical search
forever tussle between ambition, purpose, meaning;

push and pull of belonging and freedom,
doing and being,
frenzy and stillness
I thank you, Universe.

In my final breath of hours complete,
I only want to feel:
I lived. I loved. I dared.
The journey was mine.